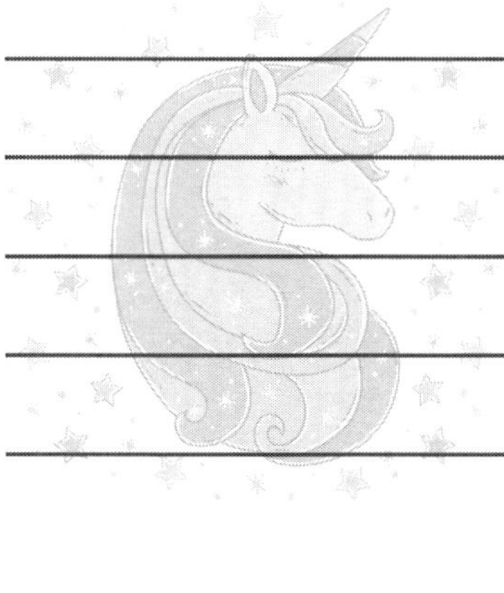

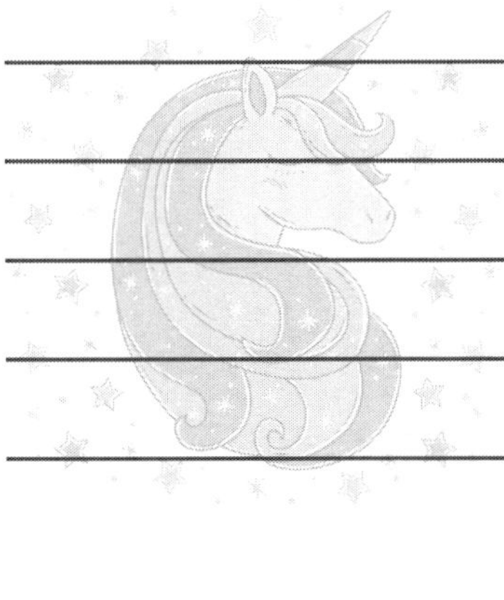

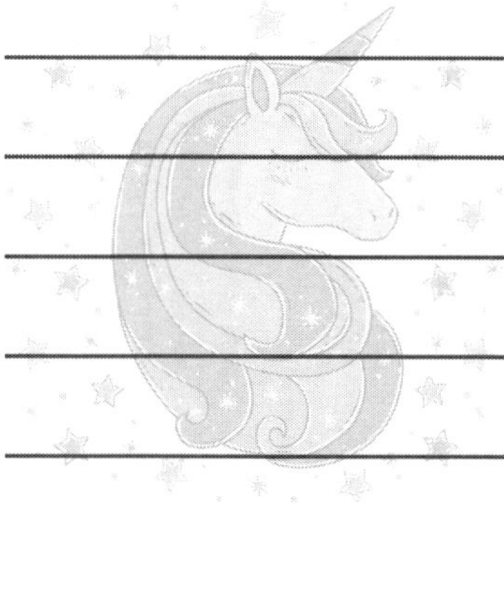

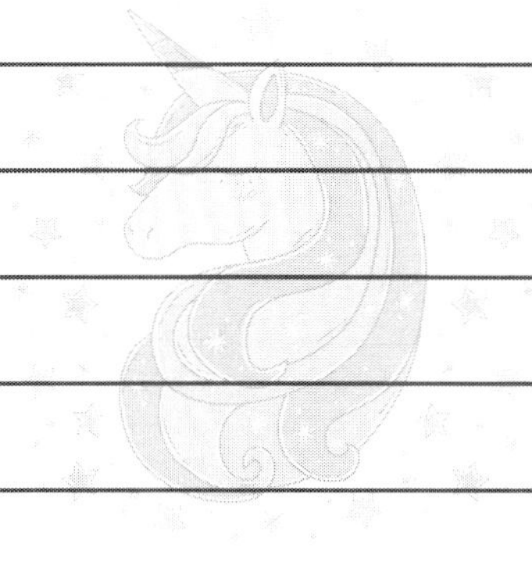

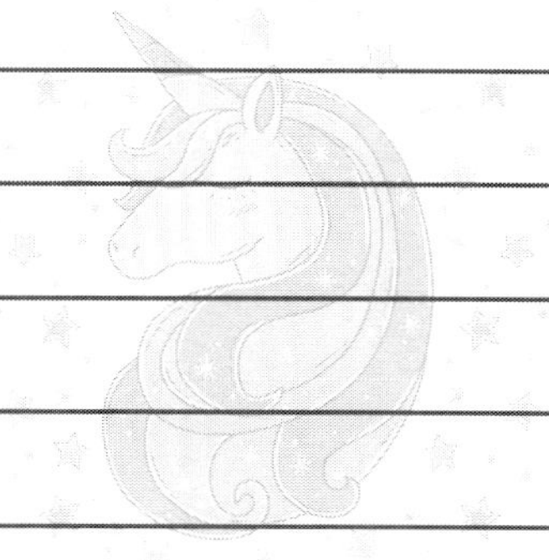

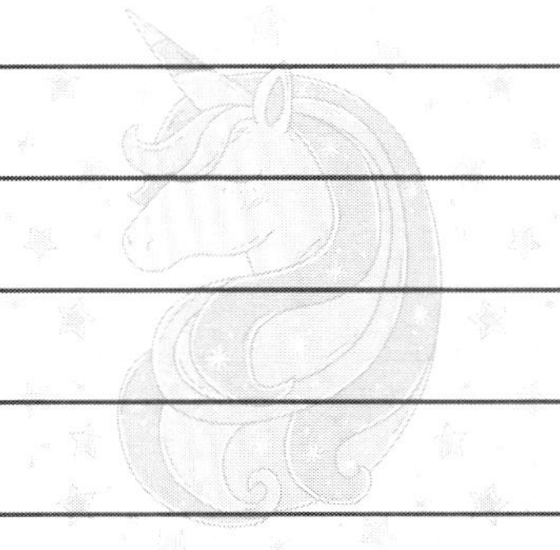

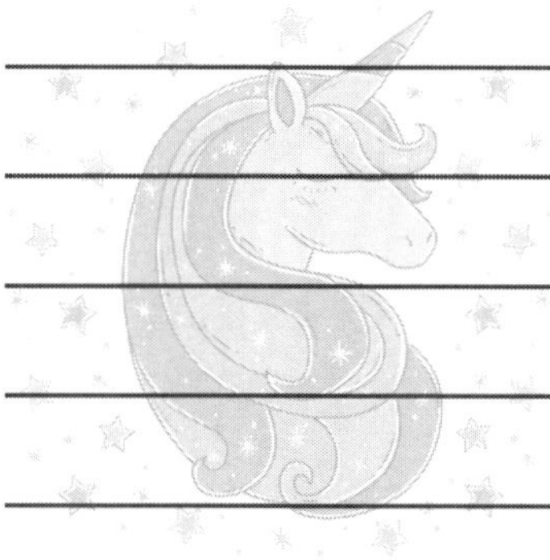

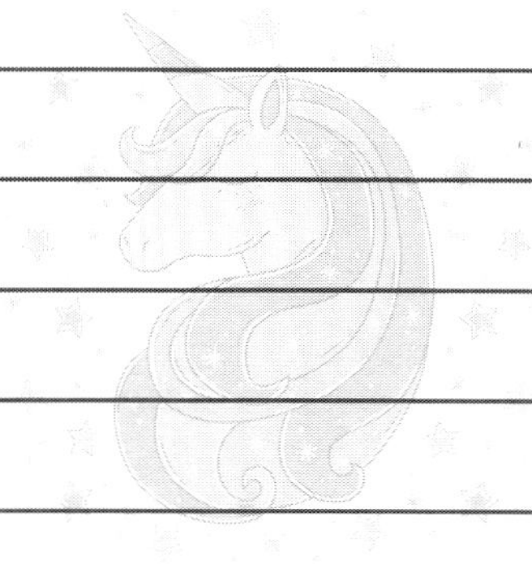

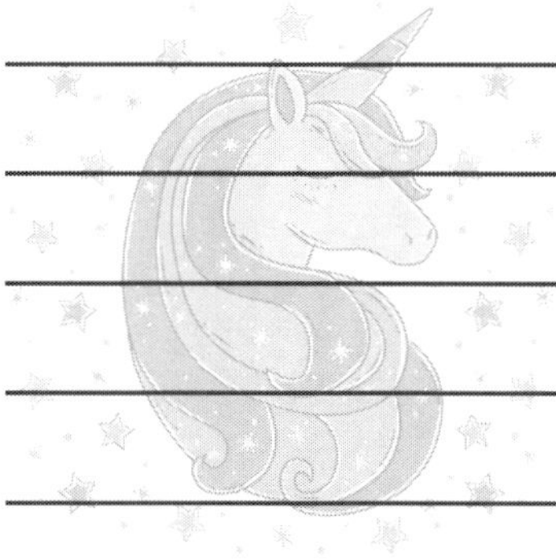

Manufactured by Amazon.ca
Acheson, AB

10773271R10074